Rapunzel

Retold by Susanna Davidson

Illustrated by
Desideria Guicciardini

Reading Consultant: Alison Kelly
University of Surrey Roehampton

Contents

Chapter 1

The witch's garden

Mr. and Mrs. Rose lived in a
small house that looked onto a
beautiful garden – a garden
they never dared enter...

...because it belonged to a wicked and powerful witch.

Mrs. Rose would sit by her window and gaze at the garden for hours.

4

But lately, she had spent a lot of time thinking about food. "Today, I'd like chocolate pudding stuffed with spinach," she decided.

Mr. Rose wasn't surprised. "Ever since you've been pregnant," he said, "you've wanted to eat the oddest things."

"Or perhaps," Mrs. Rose went on, "I'll have bananas, Brussels sprouts and, um, toothpaste. Oh yes, that would be lovely."

"Are you sure?" asked Mr. Rose.
"Yes," Mrs. Rose replied, "I am. Although I still think something might be missing..."

"Worms?" Mr. Rose suggested. "Or maybe you'd like some crushed ants on top?"

"Wait a moment!" Mrs. Rose cried, pointing to the witch's garden. "That's it."

"What is?"

"That vegetable. Oooh. It looks so green and juicy. I must have it!"

Mr. Rose looked. "Well you can't have it," he said. "I'm not going in that garden. The witch would eat me alive!"

"If I don't have that plant, I'll die," said Mrs. Rose and she began to cry.

Chapter 2

Stop thief!

I don't like heights.

After three hours of sobbing,
Mr. Rose gave in. That night,
he crept into the witch's garden.

"These vegetables all look the same in the dark," he thought. "How am I meant to know which one she wants?"

So he grabbed the nearest vegetable and raced home.

"You stupid sausage!" cried Mrs. Rose. "You've brought me a turnip. You'll have to go back again."

Next time, Mr. Rose looked carefully around the garden. "Well, this one has green leaves. It must be right!" he thought. But as he pulled it out of the ground, he shuddered. A foul smell had crept up his nose.

He looked up and
screamed. The witch was in
front of him. Mr. Rose could
smell her disgusting witchy
breath.

"How dare you steal my
rapunzel?" the witch cried.
"I'll make you pay for this,
you thieving little pimple!"

12

"I'll eat you alive," she
hissed, a nasty glint in her eye.
"I'm sure you'll be very tasty."
"P-p-please don't eat me,"
begged Mr. Rose.

He was shaking with fear.
"I was taking it for my wife.
She's about to have a b-b-
baby," he stammered.

"Hmm," said the witch, thoughtfully. "A baby?"

She paused for a moment. "I'll make a deal with you. I won't kill you and you can have as much rapunzel as you like...

Thank you, thank you.

...but you must give me the baby as soon as it's born."

Mr. Rose was so terrified, he agreed. He walked slowly home, shaking his head with worry. "Maybe she'll change her mind?" he thought, desperately.

I must hope for the best.

But as soon as his wife gave birth to their daughter, the witch appeared.

15

"The child is mine," she cried. She gave a wicked grin. "And I shall call her Rapunzel, after the plant you stole. Now, give!"

Mrs. Rose wept and wept, but the witch would not give in.

Don't take my baby.

Too late! The deal is done.

She snatched the baby, and vanished.

Chapter 3

The tower

Rapunzel lived with the witch for eleven years. She was treated like a slave.

The older she grew, the more
beautiful Rapunzel became.
She had blue eyes and long
golden hair. It flowed from the
top of her head...

down her
back...

past her
feet...

18

...and all along the ground.

"Rapunzel's getting too pretty," thought the witch. "I'll have to lock her away. I don't want any young men running off with her."

On the morning of Rapunzel's twelfth birthday, the witch woke her early.

"I have a lovely surprise for you," she said. "We're going to the forest for a picnic."

The forest was deep and dark. It didn't seem a good choice for a picnic. In the very middle of the forest stood a tower.

"I don't like it here," Rapunzel said, with a shudder.

"Get used to it," cackled the witch, "because this is your new home."

The witch cast a spell, and Rapunzel found herself in a small room, at the very top of the tower.

"I can't live here," cried Rapunzel. "There's no way out — no stairs, no door..."

"You don't need to get out," said the witch, "I just need to get in. And I can climb up your hair!"

"Maybe I won't let you," said Rapunzel.

"Then you'll starve," said the witch, with a shrug. "Come on, let's try."

Rapunzel, Rapunzel, let down your hair.

Rapunzel heaved her hair out of the window. Her long locks tumbled down the tower and landed at the witch's feet.

23

The witch climbed up
Rapunzel's hair...

...and into the tower.

Chapter 4

Prince Hans

Four years went by. Rapunzel never saw anyone, except the old witch.

And no one in the world
knew where Rapunzel was.
Until one day...

...a young and handsome
prince rode through the forest.
Rapunzel spotted him from
her window.

"Help!" she cried, as loudly as she could. "Please, help me!"

The prince looked up, astonished.

"Don't worry," he called, "I'll save you." Spurring on his horse, he galloped to the tower. "Prince Hans to the rescue!" he called.

27

He rode around the tower three times. "Um, I can't find the door," he said.

"There is no door," Rapunzel told him. "This is a magic tower. I'm being kept here by a wicked witch. You must climb up my hair."

"Well I've never done *that* before," said Prince Hans. "This is harder than it looks, you know," he added, as he began to climb.

"What's your name?" he asked.

"Rapunzel," she replied.

Prince Hans almost fell off her hair, laughing.

"Just what's so funny?" Rapunzel asked haughtily.

"You've got the same name as a vegetable!" said Prince Hans, still chuckling.

"Oh," said Rapunzel, who thought her name was rather pretty. "Perhaps I'm too *funny* to rescue?"

"Not at all," said Prince Hans, as he reached the top of the tower. "But how am I going to save you?"

"You're the prince," said Rapunzel. "You think of something."

Prince Hans looked around the room thoughtfully and spotted a pair of scissors.

"I know!" he cried, "I'll cut off your hair, make a rope and then we can both climb down it."

"You are *not* cutting off my hair," said Rapunzel. "Have you any idea how long it took to grow?"

"Fine," replied Prince Hans, "but you'll have to come up with a better idea, or your hair gets it."

Rapunzel thought quickly. "Visit me every night and bring a ball of silk with you. I'll weave a ladder from it."

"But that'll take ages," said Prince Hans.

Rapunzel frowned at him.

"...which isn't a problem," he added quickly.

After that, the prince came every evening. He told Rapunzel about his kingdom. "I live in a beautiful castle," he said. "There are courtyards full of fountains and flowers..."

And turrets that touch the sky.

Rapunzel longed to go there.

Chapter 5

The witch's trick

As the weeks passed,
Rapunzel's ladder grew longer
and longer. "Only one more
week and I'll be free..." she
thought to herself one morning.

"Rapunzel," the witch called from outside, "Rapunzel, let down your hair. I have some food for you."

As the witch climbed up, she pulled and tugged painfully on Rapunzel's hair.

"Ow!" cried Rapunzel. "Why do you always tug so much? Prince Hans never hurts me when *he* climbs."

What?!

"Prince Hans?" shouted the witch. "Who is Prince Hans? You *wicked* girl! I thought I'd shut you away from the world, but you've tricked me."

The witch leaped into the tower and quickly grabbed a pair of scissors. She hacked away at Rapunzel's hair until it lay in a heap on the floor.

"I haven't finished," cried the witch. With a powerful spell, she cast Rapunzel into the desert.

Then the witch waited for
the prince, a sly smile on her
wrinkled face.

Rapunzel,
Rapunzel! Let
down your hair.

That night, Prince
Hans called out to
Rapunzel as usual. Her
hair came shimmering down.

40

But when the prince reached the top of the tower, he gasped in shock. An ugly old crone stood in her place.

"Where's Rapunzel?" he demanded.

"Rapunzel's gone," said the witch, with a sinister laugh. "You'll never see her again."

Then the witch leaned out of the tower and kissed Prince Hans with her slimy lips.

"Yuck!" cried the prince.

It was a magic kiss. Suddenly, the prince's hands were covered in slime. He lost his grip and fell to the ground like a stone.

Prince Hans landed smack in a thorn bush. It saved his life, but the sharp thorns blinded him.

Aaargh! I can't see!

Despite his pain, Prince Hans stood up. "I may be blind," he shouted to the witch, "but I'll find Rapunzel."

"Never!" she cackled.

Prince Hans wandered for
months seeking Rapunzel.
At last, he met a camel
seller who told him about
a girl with golden hair
and blue eyes,
living alone in the
middle of the
desert.

Prince Hans hired
a driver and the fastest
horses he could find.
"Take me to the
desert," he ordered.

44

Rapunzel saw the carriage arrive in amazement. As Prince Hans stumbled out, she ran to him, put her arms around his neck and wept.

Two of her tears fell into Prince Hans' eyes, and he gasped. "I can see!" he cried.

"Rapunzel," he said, "I never thought I'd say this to a girl named after a vegetable, but will you marry me?"

"Oh yes!" said Rapunzel.

Prince Hans took Rapunzel to his castle. The entire kingdom was invited to their wedding, including Mr. and Mrs. Rose.

Princess Rapunzel and Prince Hans lived happily together for the rest of their lives and, in time, had three beautiful children – Pumpkin, Lettuce and Sprout.

Rapunzel was first written down by two brothers, Jacob and Wilhelm Grimm. They lived in Germany in the early 1800s and together they retold hundreds of fairy tales.

Series editor: Lesley Sims

Designed by
Russell Punter

First published in 2005 by Usborne Publishing Ltd., Usborne House,
83-85 Saffron Hill, London EC1N 8RT, England. www.usborne.com
Copyright © 2005 Usborne Publishing Ltd.